NOPE

T0097800

DIDN'T HAPPEN
of the **YEAR AWARDS**

#DHOTYA

VISIT US ON TWITTER @_DHOTYA

CONTENTS

First edition printed in 2022 in the UK
ISBN: 978-1-915538-00-0

Compiled by: Harry Barnes
Edited by: Emily Readman, Katie Fisher
Designed by: Paul Cocker
Sales & PR: Emma Toogood, Lizzy Capps
Contributors: Lis Ellis, Lizzie Morton

me:ze
PUBLISHING

Published by Meze Publishing Limited
Unit 1b, 2 Kelham Square
Kelham Riverside
Sheffield S3 8SD
Web: www.mezepublishing.co.uk
Telephone: 0114 275 7709
Email: info@mezepublishing.co.uk

Printed in the UK by Bell and Bain Ltd, Glasgow

INTRODUCTION

Welcome to the Didn't Happen of the Year Awards (DHOTYA) - The Book. Amazingly, somehow, this book is something that has actually happened, although I'm self-aware enough to realise that a Twitter account that just says "didn't happen" in a hundred different ways a year has no right to be sold for £9.99 anywhere.

Apparently though, there's enough of you who find that funny, which is great otherwise this would be a waste of a lot of people's time.

Over the course of the next 100 or so pages, you'll find a compilation of the best DHOTYA entries of all time, dating back to the start in 2016, along with the original fan interaction on the majority of the posts, which is always my favourite part of the account, rather than the actual content itself. I also asked the DHOTYA followers for their favourite personal stories which, if seen online, were so outrageous that they could feature on the account - I've included my own favourites in this book too.

I've tried to capture what have been some quite iconic Twitter moments for the DHOTYA followers, including the meltdown of Tom Zanetti, me being called out for a fight by Chris Eubank, Conservative MP Owen Paterson writing an official letter-headed letter to Labour MP Louise Haigh demanding she withdraws her nomination of him for DHOTYA, and lots of other great moments.

For those that don't follow the Twitter account and have just found this book in the bargain bin of WH Smith for 99p, you might find it useful to know how the account works. All year long, people tag DHOTYA in their favourite posts on the internet where they're calling bullshit. Tagging DHOTYA is a playful way of saying "I don't believe you". I'll then pick my favourites, where I think the followers will enjoy it, and post them.

The best 32 at the end of the year make it to the annual awards in December which will usually run for three days. This is where the fun really starts, as they'll be randomly divided into eight groups of four, just like a football World Cup format. On day one of the awards, followers get the chance to vote for their favourite DHOTYA post in each of the eight groups, and the two entries in each group with the most votes progress to day two of the awards (knocking out the two with the least votes in each group), leaving 16 entries. Those 16 entries will then face each other in a 1v1 knockout vote, until the quarter final, semi final, final and eventually a winner is decided.

Very uniquely, the annual awards have a betting market hosted by BetVictor (although sporadically there have been other bookmakers offering odds), where punters can have a small bet on their favourite, usually to a maximum of £10, to add some extra fun for those who want to. Contrary to popular belief, I don't make a single penny from people losing bets so each year I genuinely take the side of the followers. The annual market from BetVictor is the first time a bookmaker via an affiliation has offered odds on the outcome of a social media poll in social media history. Some could argue there's a small exception where the Betfair Exchanges offered odds on Richard Osman's "World Cup" polls previously, but this is fan-to-fan betting rather than an affiliation with a bookies and isn't comparing like-for-like.

Why the book? Well, I've always been keen not to "sell out" when it comes to DHOTYA, so I've tried my hardest not to ruin the account by monetising it too much with ads and merch, only really generating an income from things that actually fit the content well. Over the years there have been a lot of requests for merch from followers, and I've been at a crossroads as to whether to trust my own judgement or to give those followers what they want. After a couple of publishers reaching out in 2022 to do this book, I took Meze Publishing up on their offer and here we are!

It'd be great to get people's feedback on this book, because after spending months collating content for it and balancing this with my normal life, I'm so involved in it now that I won't be able to judge properly if it's any good, so send @_DHOTYA a tweet or a DM with honest opinions. If you like it, maybe an annual book of the previous year's content could be on the cards.

ABOUT THE AUTHOR

Imagine being asked to write a bio about yourself. I've tried to subtly ignore the publisher over the last few months every time I've been asked to do this section, hoping it'd be forgotten about but here I am, four weeks before the release date, losing that battle.

So basically, I'm Harry and I'm the guy behind the @_DHOTYA Twitter account. If you've followed the account for a while you might know that I'm not the guy who started DHOTYA, but instead I'm the person who's taken it from a small account to the funny or annoying (depending which side you're on) Twitter presence that it is today.

I actually bought the account in January 2018, when it was a year old at 17k followers, for £250 + £50 if I could grow the account to 80k followers by the end of 2018… it reached 112k by the end of that year, so I paid a total of £300. Why? Well, this isn't an autobiography so I won't bore you with the exact thought process, but long story short, reaching over a quarter of a billion people per year, organically and for free, as DHOTYA does, is quite a valuable tool.

You're not likely to see me trying to turn social media into a full time job, despite the fact that I have a platform where I could do so, because I'm pretty weird and love my "normal" corporate career too much, but I think you'll definitely keep seeing me doing random stuff like DHOTYA, or The State of LinkedIn and other bits as a hobby.

Look, if you're a normal 26 year old lad from a working class background and you tell people you're getting a publishing deal for a book, the first thing someone says is not "congratulations", it's "oh my god can I be in it?".

I feel I owe a very specific shoutout to one friend, Brooke Smedley, who has been a massive help with the initial set up of another account of mine, The State of LinkedIn. He has since gone on to pretty much run that by himself and will soon find himself doing social media full time as he's building his own very well-respected brand.

Right, here we go…

Family

Mum

Linda Saunders

Dennis Saunders

Christie Barnes

James Barnes

Dad

Ryan Golding

Daniel Golding

Liam Golding

Amy Golding

Daniel Hogg

Stella Hogg

Claire Hepple

Friends

Charlotte Davies

Olivia Davies

Lucy Wright

Bradley Alcock

Kyle Caruana

Shannon Holtom

Jade Brittain

Megan Kaziow

Nicky Kennan

Neal Coopey

John Onikute

Jay Flaherty

Shannon Quinlan

Ed O'Connor

Brooke Smedley

Sheldon Waite

Billy Hulott

Bailey Mussell

Jack Brownridge

THAT'S
NEWS
TO ME

As a DHOTYA follower, there's nothing more interesting than when shit hits the fan in the news. This is usually when something political kicks off, such as Brexit, a US presidential election or a UK general election. Covid had a big part to play, too.

A lot of DHOTYA entries confuse people because they often wonder: "Why would you make this up?". With the topical posts, however, you can often see an obvious agenda. Whether it's to insult your political opposition, show off your own perceived intelligence, or just to wind up Twitter, you usually see the worst of people when it comes to current events.

Personally, I know I'm being unbiased when I'm getting insulted by both ends of the political spectrum. One day I'll be getting accused of being on Jeremy Corbyn's payroll, and the next I'll be getting called a "Tory c***". Imagine being that angry at the Didn't Happen of the Year Awards…

DONALD TRUMP

I WON THIS ELECTION, BY A LOT!

Donald Trump via Twitter, @realDonaldTrump

*Official sources may not have called the race when this was Tweeted

It's been hard not to make DHOTYA all about Donald Trump, or at least between the key years of 2017-2020. I'd class myself as relatively central politically, so I'm probably not as hysterical about Trump as a lot of people are, but there's definitely a case for his Twitter, while he was President, being nominated for DHOTYA.

I wanted to approach this book similarly to how I run DHOTYA and not focus too much on one politician, party or ideology. You've got to take the piss out of all sides as much as possible, so with that in mind, I thought I'd single out just one Trump tweet.

Although there are some outrageous tweets that are much more "What the fuck is he on about?", the imagery and simplicity behind this one just can't be beaten. Not only did he claim to win the election "by a lot" at the exact moment it was confirmed he'd lost, but the tweet was also flagged by Twitter for its possible inaccuracy (a feature Twitter introduced pretty much because of Trump himself).

My secret ambition for DHOTYA was to be noticed by Trump, who undoubtedly had the immaturity and impulsivity to try and use it to disprove Hillary Clinton or call out "fake news CNN". Your early twenties aren't typically known for having lots of peak moments, especially if you haven't met somebody or had any kids yet, but having the President of the United States of America publicly use you to beat down his "enemies" would've been a difficult one to top.

COSTING HUMANS

Talked to my daughter (8) about the covid situation this morning.

She said "It's just like climate change. They won't do anything because they say it's too expensive, but it will end up costing humans."

She's more correct than she knows, the parallel's run deeper.

Kit Yates @Kit_Yates_Maths

Chielini Lookout @chielinilookout
Replying to @Kit_Yates_Maths

As soon as he opened the bracket I wonder how long he thought about what age this imaginary character is. Somehow settled it with 8. Madness.

B

Brose @Brose1878
Replying to @Kit_Yates_Maths

And the greenhouse gases clapped.

Anthiochus @BrianOrsdel
Replying to @Kit_Yates_Maths

My cat asked: "Why is there something rather than nothing?" And I said: "Did you really shit on my dads pillow again Professor Paw?" We both laughed. And I took my meds.

I don't have a cat."

I had a mask on and walked into a jammed post office. A guy was leaving, approaching the doors as I entered.
He looked at me and muttered loudly "Fucking sheep," and I hollered back "Nobody wants to hear about your hobbies."
The entire PO exploded in laughter.
A few folks clapped.

Go Deep, I'll Look For You @MattSchultz13

Jack R @Jack_R93
Replying to @MattSchultz13

Why do they always have to add in that people clapped?!

Sir Wan T @SDM250567
Replying to @MattSchultz13

We might need a new category Didn't Happen Of The Year But We Wished It Did Award (DHOTYBWWIDA).

It's a bit of a mouthful mind yoh.

Ian @mufcmad10
Replying to @MattSchultz13

To be fair though, thats a cracking joke …

Didn't happen, but is deffo a funny.

NICKI MINAJ

My cousin in Trinidad won't get the vaccine cuz his friend got it & became impotent. His testicles became swollen. His friend was weeks away from getting married, now the girl called off the wedding. So just pray on it & make sure you're comfortable with ur decision, not bullied

Nicki Minaj via Twitter, @NICKIMINAJ

Nicki @nickicov
Replying to @NICKIMINAJ

Imagine being outed by Nicki Minaj for your STD 😷😷😷 This is why I'm the only Nicki to be trusted with your secrets, I got less followers to tell…

Ken Barlow @I_am_KenBarlow
Replying to @NICKIMINAJ

Don't scoff. The same thing happened to me. I had the vaccine, and now one of my bollocks is much bigger than the other two.

Ryan @Ryan_Gooner97
Replying to @NICKIMINAJ

Fair play to her for outing a family friend for most likely catching an STD.

Think he might be single now for other reasons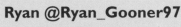

This one from Nicki Minaj didn't really need my help going viral for being bullshit: it reached over 150k likes before I'd even been able to screenshot it. Let's be honest, Nicki Minaj has a much bigger following than I'll ever have, so she doesn't need my help going viral for anything.

I never had Nicki down as being a Laurence Fox type, so I have a bit of sympathy for her here. I think she'd heard a story from a friend and just believed it, but deep down I think we all know that her cousin's friend probably caught an STD from cheating and didn't want to admit it.

"It was the vaccine, babe, I swear!"

STAMPING A CRUTCH

Oh my days 😂 no joke, I took the mrs to Asda in Nuneaton earlier and she's still sad about the Queen dying (RIP) and had a t shirt on with the Queens face.

Stood in the queue to pay and the worker stood up and saluted her and started singing God Save the King 😳 😳 next thing you know everyone and I mean EVERYONE in Asda started joining in and the whole store started belting the national anthem.

Everyone around me started clapping (except this one lad on crutches but he was stamping a crutch) and you could tell the lad servicing us had a pure tear in his eye. I fuckin love this country man. 🫡🇬🇧

Anon via Facebook

R Rosie @Rosie94008268
Replying to Anon

This has everything. Patriotism, clapping, ASDA, tears.
A thing of beauty.

J James E @jimmy1shoe
Replying to Anon

There was a lad 'servicing' them? I didn't realise things like that went on in supermarkets 😂

F Felix Moss @FeeMossy
Replying to Anon

Big hint, when someone starts off something with "no joke" chances are it's a joke.

I came across my first actual anti-masker today in my local Co-Op. She was wanging on about how they don't work anyway blaa blaa.

Everyone was a bit uncomfortable waiting in line, then my 3 year old yelled: "WHY IS THAT STUPID LADY NOT WEARING A MASK UGH! THERE ARE JUST SO MANY DICK HEADS IN THIS SHOP."

There was a silence, then lots of laughter, I felt sorry for the poor cashier lady trying to keep it together.

Anti mask lady just muttered and left.

Amy Stockton, Facebook

 Andreas Gündüz @andreastweeted
Replying to Amy Stockton

Why would you fabricate that you have taught your 3 yo child to swear and be abusive to strangers in public?

 Trizzer @trizzer3
Replying to Amy Stockton

The child went onto explain that the use of swear words is a sign of intelligence and a well place swear word can add much needed emphasis. 😂

 Matt Barron @VonBarronshire
Replying to Amy Stockton

And then the CoOp gave me free shopping for a year and my 3 year old was given a guard of honour on the way out of the automatic doors

NORMAL PEOPLE

This chapter title is probably a bit misleading - most "normal" people don't post such bollocks on the internet, but they're probably the most normal people out of all of the ones featured in this book.

One of my personal favourites is in here too: #WokeCup. I still remember the first time I saw this. I knew immediately it would go down well in DHOTYA history, and I reckon it's one of the purest DHOTYA entries of all time.

I have to laugh though, as I've become very desensitized to this type of post because of how long I've been running DHOTYA. I actually feel sorry for the editor(s) of this book who, as far as I know, had never seen DHOTYA before editing it, and have had to hand-type the posts word for word. They've probably just read "Miss Kingston" and started re-evaluating their career choice.*

*Editor: Yes, Harry. Yes, I have.

PASSPORT

So I got to the airport this morning to take the next flight to UK, then I realize I forgot my passport at home, still thinking of what to do, this pilot saw me and was like am I not ameenah from Twitter, I said yes, long story short, I am now tweeting from the UK.

Tweeted by @ammeenat on 20/03/2022

Didn't Happen of the Year Awards @_DHOTYA
Replying to @ammeenat

One of the worst I've seen.

ThisCouldBeAnyone @MansoonT
Replying to @ammeenat

...and then all the planes started clapping

Zelensky Fan Club @AkbarFazel
Replying to @ammeenat

Well actually, I'm that pilot and I had a fatal heart attack and she single handedly landed the plane ... whilst tweeting ... honest.

At the time of writing this (July 2022), this is my favourite entry of 2022 so far, and I really think it could go on to win the awards this year.

It's a perfect entry: it's just mindless bullshit with literally no purpose. No political agenda, no self-promo of a new product or book, no trying to make out like your toddler is a genius. Just pure, unimaginative bullshit with no end goal. Glorious.

I really do think that by the time you've bought and read this, it'll have won DHOTYA 2022. If not, either something unreal has come up post-July 2022, or the awards have gone to shit!

CREME EGG

New Cadbury promotion is a Creme Egg that's half white chocolate, half milk chocolate. Found one (bought from ASDA). Opened it in store. Old lady walks up to me (unaware it's worth £10,000) and says "Oh I love the combination of milk and white, where was that from young man?" and, not wanting to break her heart, I just gave it to her. Good deed for the day done.

Anon is feeling positive, via Facebook

 Ayden Callaghan @AydenCallaghan:
Replying to Anon

Then Klopp saw him playing down the park and said get your boots son, you're playing on Saturday.

 GreenGoldDevils @GoldDevils20:
Replying to Anon

Liverpool fan, what else can we expect!

MISS KINGSTON

Remember this one time in Year 10 I got caught wanking thorough my pockets in the back of class by my Maths teacher Miss Kingston.

She looked at me, looked at my bulge, winked at me, bit her lip and told me to be quick with it. Wouldn't mind but she was in her 50's but used that image to fuel me for years.

Anon, via Facebook

Steve @_AstralWeeks
Replying to Anon

It's a Busted/Inbetweeners collaboration this.

Kai @HerrTod_
Replying to Anon

The rest of the class applauded and sang the national anthem quick afterwards.

Skooma Junkie @LilGucciMole
Replying to Anon

Some Jay from the inbetweeners shit that.

Adam Reilly @adsreilly
Replying to Anon

To be fair. I remember when I got caught wanking at school in a Maths lesson. I was never allowed to teach again!

CREAMFIELDS

Em
@Emmakkkay

Helped myself to a free pint behind the bar and the security came over and said 'Ay get me one'.

Replying to @Jemimawand1

> **Jemima @Jemimawand1**
> Did creamfields employ security this year or not?

This is a fairly basic entry, and not one of the most naturally popular ones. Then again, it does resonate with anybody who went to Creamfields in 2021, and even more so with those that go regularly.

Security at Creamfields is usually ridiculously tight, probably rightfully so considering 90% of the people there are on Ket. But in 2021, Pablo Escobar could have walked in with a wheelbarrow full of coke and security would've just waved him through (as long as he didn't have canned deodorant with him, anyway.)

That being said, stealing pints from the bar in front of security and having them ask you for one isn't very likely, and it might just be a step too far in the Creamfields 2021 folklore.

#WOKECUP

Popped on the World Cup to see Russia were playing Saudi Arabia…

10-yr-old: "I don't know who to support here, dad. Who's got the better human rights record?"

#WokeCup

Tweeted by Be Ben Stevens @stephens_ben

James Prosho @jdprosho
Replying to @stephens_ben

It's eternally more likely that his 10 year old said "Why the fuck are you at home during the day? Get out and get a job."

Chris_Healy @Chris_Healy
Replying to @stephens_ben

Surely outright winner already! @_DHOTYA

Unfair to add him to the competition. Everyone else is playing for second place!

Martin Boot @MartinBooth_
Replying to @stephens_ben

Put your feet up, mate. That won't be beaten in the next six-and-a-half months.

This is my personal favourite.

It's such a simple, effective lie, and it epitomises everything DHOTYA is about. This is probably the clearest example of a "Purist" DHOTYA entry, including a woke child, an unpredictable quote, and a catchy hashtag.

I remember seeing this for the first time on my lunch break at work, and I knew immediately that it would do well with DHOTYA's followers. As soon as it was posted, its engagement was showing better numbers than any I'd ever seen, and people's reactions were incredible.

Ben Stephens, the author of the post and a seemingly "normal" Twitter user, has persistently claimed that this interaction with his son did happen in exactly this way. He even replied to DHOTYA followers about it and engaged in numerous debates and arguments.

Interestingly, this was the first time I'd considered the impact of having a large following on Twitter, which was something I'd never experienced before nor really considered the dangers of. Previously, popular interactions had come from celebrities or people that made a conscious effort to be in the spotlight, but this was the first time that a "normal" person had an entry that blew up. It was the first time we saw the human side to being nominated.

Being completely honest, my opinion then was (and still is, but now in a much more mature and conscious way) that if you tweet to the public, the public have a right to react. Sometimes you'll like it, sometimes you won't. This was, however, the foundation of being more conscious of the author of these posts and, as the years have gone on and the followers have gone up, I have considered my actions much more greatly, and taken extreme care and consideration before each post.

In my opinion, this should have gone further than the semi-finals in 2018, and I'll never forgive the public for not getting this into the final. Should've known you couldn't be trusted with a vote after Chico got as far as he did in The X Factor back in 2005.

A
QUESTIONABLE
SPORT

You'd have thought that sport didn't really provide many possible entries to DHOTYA: bad opinions and lots of emotions maybe, but not really a DHOTYA moment. At least nothing on the level of Tory-hating 3-year-olds and 8-year-old human rights advocates, anyway.

That's where you're wrong. It's sometimes the sportspeople or the clubs themselves that are the actual problem, not just their fans. Everything from football clubs being excited about the DHOTYA group draw to a surprising claim to being the fastest woman alive, this chapter is a weirdly interesting one.

Sorry if you're a Villa supporter reading this, too.

ASTON VILLA FC

Birmingham Library last night. 😍😍😍
#TheCityIsOurs #AVFC

Aston Villa FC, @AVFCOfficial via Twitter

 Aston Villa ✔
@AVFCOfficial

Birmingham Library last night. 😍

#TheCityIsOurs #AVFC

12:45 · 28/05/2019 · Twitter for iPhone

Photo:
@AVFCOfficial

Luke @LukeMartyn89
Replying to @AVFCOfficial

Then the entire library silently applauded.

Kristian Clark @Kristianclark1
Replying to @AVFCOfficial

Birmingham City Library last night...

Simon Powell @MrSimonPowell
Replying to @AVFCOfficial

We wish it could be Xmas every day.

ASTON VILLA FC

This Aston Villa post makes me laugh because it's clearly just an error from the Villa admin.

For anybody who hasn't got a good enough eye to spot it, this tweet is dated 28th May 2019, and it suggests that the posted photo was taken only the day before. The Library of Birmingham lit up in Aston Villa colours: seems fine, right? Well, for starters, there's a Christmas tree outside the library in this image, and despite what they say about Birmingham - it's actually a nice city that I go to a lot - there are no Christmas trees up in May.

So this goes one of two ways: either the Aston Villa admin was flat-out lying and thought he'd get away with it, or, more likely, they used the wrong picture.

Well, the good news is that I was already connected

with the Villa Twitter admin on LinkedIn, although I don't think I'd actually spoken with him at this point. Naturally, I went into his DMs to find out what was going on. I don't share the specifics of DMs, but the Villa admin did admit that it was an honest mistake.

He told me that the Library of Birmingham was in fact lit up in Villa colours that night, but they didn't have a photo of it, so he used one they already had. Unluckily for him, he hadn't clocked the Christmas tree outside the building and just posted it. There was also an admission that, once called out by DHOTYA, he'd considered coming back with some banter, but worried he'd lose in the long run.

Here I was thinking that my club, Manchester United, were the banter club...

PELÉ

Once, in a match in Senegal, the goalkeeper cried so much after I scored that he had to be substituted! He had lost a big bet! 🪦

Pelé via Twitter, @Pele

Pelé ✓
@Pele

Once, in a match in Senegal, the goalkeeper cried so much after I scored that he had to be substituted! He had lost a big bet! 🔲// Em uma partida em Senegal, eu lembro que o goleiro chorou tanto depois do gol que ele teve que ser substituído. Ele perdeu uma grande aposta! 🔲

Photo:
@Pele

It's hard to believe anything football legend Pelé says when his goalscoring record changes every time he talks about it. He seems to add goals scored during his primary school lunchtimes and training matches into his overall records.

We all know Pelé is an icon and an unbelievable footballer, but it's the undocumented periods of his career that seem to be his best work.

This particular entry to DHOTYA was just a very random post: a previously unheard story with no context behind it. Is he trying to drop the fact that there were efforts to fix the match? No idea, but it's a very suspicious post from Pelé. It was never strong enough to win the end of year awards, but it was definitely worthy of a shoutout in the competition.

BRITNEY SPEARS

Ran my first 5!!!! Getting over your fear of pushing it in the beginning is key …. once I did that I hit 5!!!!! Usually I run 6 or 7 …. my first try was 9 …. and now I did it whoop!!!!! 100 meter dash 🏃🕸️🤍🤍😔

Britney Spears via Instagram, @britneyspears

britneyspears

00:05.97

Reset ● ● Start

Lap 1 00:05.97

♡ ○ ◁ 🔖

Liked by **oneofthosefaces** and **27,367 others**

britneyspears Ran my first 5 !!!! Getting over your fear of pushing it in the beginning is key …. once I did that I hit 5 !!!!! Usually I run 6 or 7 …. my first try was 9 …. and now I did it whoop !!!!! 100 meter dash 🏃🌸💕😅 !!!!!

Photo: @BritneySpears

Jimmy Jackson @Jjacko_1
Replying to @britneyspears

I see @_DHOTYA anti female agenda is still going strong.

Just because it's a 40 year old, female singer you automatically assume she cannot run approximately twice as fast as the previous fastest human on the planet.

Shame on you!

Dylan Vella @dcvkeeper3
Replying to @britneyspears

And she did it in 9 seconds on her FIRST TRY!

Steve Nicholas @stevenicholas00
Replying to @britneyspears

Bullshit me baby one more time.

ApThirteen @apthirteen
Replying to @britneyspears

Photo:
@apthirteen

BRITNEY SPEARS

There was nothing funnier in lockdown than the day Britney Spears claimed she'd done the 100m sprint in 5.97 seconds - nearly 40% faster than Usain Bolt - in her back garden.

As well as the bold claim that she'd broken his world record, Britney went on to say that she usually ran it in six or seven seconds, casually breaking Bolt's record of 9.58 seconds pretty much every time she bothered trying.

This would've been funny no matter who claimed it, but to hear it from Britney Spears of all people...

We all needed a lift at that point in the pandemic, and the post came at a time when people were posting the craziest 5km run times, so it really gave us all a chance to laugh.

I don't think Britney ever came out and corrected herself, so we can all just accept and agree that Britney is the fastest human on the planet. What a woman.

WAYNE HENNESSEY

Yesterday evening I had a meal with my team mates and we had a group photograph.

I waved and shouted at the person taking the picture to get on with it and at the same time put my hand over my mouth to make the sound carry.

It's been brought to my attention that frozen in a moment by the camera this looks like I am making a completely inappropriate type of salute.

I can assure everyone I would never ever do that and any resemblance to that kind of gesture is absolutely coincidental.

Love and peace

Wayne.

Wayne Hennessey via Twitter, @WayneHennessey1

Bill Sergeant @BillSergeant2
Replying to @WayneHennessey1

Worth noting the player taking the photo was Max Meyer - the only German in the squad. There's no squirming out of this one.

James White @Buttscratcher
Replying to @WayneHennessey1

Imagine winning this in the first week. Incredible effort from Wayne. Really set the bar high for the remaining 11 and 3/4 months.

Len @len_shayler
Replying to @WayneHennessey1

Genuinely think this is a winner already.

CHELSEA FC

Maurizio Sarri says the Kepa substitution confusion was 'a big misunderstanding' because he thought the player had cramp. However he says Kepa was right that he could continue although the way he went about it was wrong. Sarri says he needs to talk to Kepa now. #CHEMCI

Chelsea FC via Twitter @ChelseaFC

Clappers @Clappertron
Replying to @ChelseaFC

Between this, Hennessy and Eubank I feel sports should have a separate category from the rest as it's getting ridiculous now.

MyNameIsDave @ObiWanDave
Replying to @ChelseaFC

Gotta be the winner for 2019. We all watched it on TV for fuck sake.

Matt_ @mattyL313
Replying to @ChelseaFC

It's the oscars tonight as well.

In isolation, this is a regular tweet of a statement by Chelsea's then-manager, Maurizio Sarri. However, with the added context that everyone had seen Kepa, the Chelsea goalkeeper, refuse to be substituted in the League Cup final, Sarri's statement and the subsequent tweet comfortably fell into DHOTYA territory.

Though topical and funny at the time of its posting in February 2019, nobody felt it'd go very far in the DHOTYA awards that year, and it nearly missed the cut. When it made it into the final 32, there was a feeling it'd naturally drop out early on without much fuss.

However, after tweeting the draw, which showed

CHELSEA FC

Chelsea's entry in the same group as Rebekah Vardy's "Denial" entry, the official Chelsea FC Twitter account responded with the comment "Tough group", right in the middle of announcing the December fixtures. Their tweet went on to reach over 40,000 likes and was picked up by a number of major UK newspapers.

On a personal level, I couldn't believe what I was reading. DHOTYA was being exposed to millions of people around the world, and there was even a chance that Chelsea's players would read the tweet - in complete bewilderment - and take a look at the account. I did hope for a few more footballers to follow DHOTYA on the back of it, but that never really materialised. Still, I was so excited by this tweet, and it's probably one of my personal highlights.

I quickly found the Social Media Editor who had posted the tweet on LinkedIn (I'll keep his name private because I'm not sure if he wants a mention) and we talked about the post, how positively it had been engaged with, and shared links to the news articles that were coming out about it. Again, I don't like to share specific details of private DMs, but all I'll really say is that it doesn't seem to be something that Chelsea regretted posting. Quite the opposite.

As a Manchester United fan though, I still hope Chelsea get relegated. Sorry. (I'm not actually sorry.)

GLENN TAMPLIN

> Shopping in Nike Dubai and the staff recognised us and couple them showed me they follow Billericay and wanted pictures Billericay like it or not becoming known WORLDWIDE and we still in our first year 💪💪💪💪👏👏👏👏🦁🦁🦁🦁
>
> Glenn Tamplin via Twitter @glenntamplin

Shopping in Nike Dubai and the staff recognised us and couple them showed me they follow Billericay and wanted pictures

Billericay like it or not becoming known WORLDWIDE and we still in our first year

Photo: @glenntamplin

Most of you reading this won't know who Glenn Tamplin is, nor the interaction DHOTYA had with him at the start of 2018. Although Glenn will be convinced you do know him, you might just want to quickly close the book and Google who he is.

Glenn is the former owner and, I believe, manager of Billericay Town Football Club, a non-league football club in, well, Billericay. For those not into football, it's a semi-pro team a good number of leagues below the Premier League. Being involved in non-league Coventry United myself at the time, I remember seeing Glenn and Billericay Town become a bit of a laughing stock in the non-league scene because of Glenn's weird antics and that really cringe changing room wall they had. YouTube will likely have some videos that can show you what I'm on about.

My gut feeling is that Glenn is smarter than he comes across, and that he was probably just playing the part of a pantomime villain, wanting to bring attention to Billericay Town and himself through being controversial, arrogant, and a bit cocky. It's very similar to what I suspect Tom Zanetti does, where deep down I'm sure they're both nice enough guys.

But, let's be honest, nobody in Dubai has a clue who Glenn or Billericay Town is, and you know for a fact that Glenn asked the Nike store workers for that photo. When he was called out, Glenn went on the defensive and kicked off like a naughty child. Ultimately, it resulted in him blocking DHOTYA - sad times. Since then, people who knew who he was had forgotten his existence until reading this page.

PROFOUND
NONSENSE

This is one of my favourite chapters in the book: it's basically just full of absolute bullshit with no purpose other than showing off how amazing the authors or their children are, and how shit the rest of us should feel...

SUPER BOWL

Me to 8-y-o: Who do you want to win, the Bengals or the Rams?

8-y-o: What difference does it make? It's not like the winner is going to solve climate change.

Super Bowl weekend in the Scheiber-Sullivan household got heavy real quick...

Noam Scheiber @noamscheiber

S **Steve Kray @StevieConkSU**
Replying to @noamscheiber

Dude, if you were to ask me what team is going to win, when I was like 8 I would just say the team with a colour I like more lmao

---

S **SMcC @StMcC90**
Replying to @noamscheiber

He put his Mrs surname last too... 😂😂

E **Eoin @kkkeelers**
Replying to @noamscheiber

This is true, I was the climate.

On a train. As I usually am. Heavily tattooed guy (up his neck) wearing (strangely) fingerless gloves. Biker Gang look. Next to him was the only spare seat. People were standing up to avoid sitting there. I sat down. He nodded at me. Then his phone rang. I felt everyone tense up. Was this the call instructing him to go berserk? Get his nunchucks out? He answered;

"Hey Mum. Yeah I'm off to see Gran now. I'll stay there until the carer gets there. You want me to pick up some dinner?"

Smirks across the carriage. People cross with themselves for such a huge assumption. We must not judge books by their covers. Simply ever.

Joe Jones via LinkedIn

Smirks is a lovely entry to be fair, if it had actually happened. I actually kinda hope it did happen, but it just seems too cliché. Bit of an Aesop's Fable type vibe from this post though, and with it being posted to LinkedIn there's a 99% chance that it's only been posted to brownnose his boss, probably just before a pay review.

Either way, this never really lived up to a huge amount of hype in the end of year awards; the competition was just too strong.

CHILLS

I asked my 10yo today how he was going to remember how to spell financial on his spelling test.

"C as in chills. As in the chills you get when you find out the government is removing financial support from those who need it."

I can finish parenting now, right??

Anonymous, via Twitter

Mark S @markqpr1969
Replying to anonymous

My kid is 12...... he didn't say f*** all 'cos he's too busy staring at the TV playing Fortnite. Proud Dad.

Phil James @PhilWrightson
Replying to anonymous

Before you finish parenting maybe tell your kid that financial doesn't start with a c. That'll give him chills too.

We got our 6yo son a new Switch for xmas. Went to the park today. He played with another boy who also had their Switch with them. He came over to me and I noticed one of his controllers was a different colour. He explained to me that his new friend Tariq had two Brown controllers and he had two White controllers. They each agreed that their Switchs didn't represent the world of equality that they wanted to live in so they swapped one controller with each other so they now have one Brown and one White now. Was so proud of him, gave him a big hug and looked across the park.... saw Tariq's mum giving him a big hug too and we both started crying. Parenting is it's own reward.

Anonymous, via Facebook

Ben @bena_324
Replying to anonymous

I'm Tariq's mother, I can confirm.

EnglandFlags @AllEnglandFlags
Replying to anonymous

And the pigeons in the park all clapped

C Bolx @crankybolx
Replying to anonymous

All the ppl saying you can't get brown controllers..? You can, I have one.

Photo: @crankybolx

"Everyone dies one day. Everyone. Even wolves. But not books. Not words. Words don't die."
My son, 3, who is a lot smarter than I am.

Rebecca Hazleton via Twitter, @hinxminx

Tartankoala @tartankoala
Replying to @hinxminx

I read this tweet to my 3yo son.

"The robust yet pungent whiff of bovine excrement tantalises my olfactory organ" says he.

"Eh?"

"I smell bullshit pater, BULL. SHIT." he replied.

Charl @charsenal10
Replying to @hinxminx

Is it a coincidence that 90% of the DHOTYA nominees are authors/writers who "happen" to have publications that they want to plug

Stephen Ford @1em0nhead
Replying to @hinxminx

Just delete your account now DHOTYA; this wont be beaten. World record on our hands.

DO YOU WANT A FIGHT?

This chapter is a golden one. Every now and then, you'll find that being nominated for DHOTYA really gets under the skin of some people, and these people haven't learned that the internet finds it funny when they go into meltdown over something so trivial.

From Chris Eubank offering to fight me after claiming he won the lottery, to Tom Zanetti DM'ing me videos of him on a helicopter to justify calling a railway employee a "jellybean", there have been some weird interactions.

These interactions are often what a lot of people remember DHOTYA for, and when DHOTYA is all done and dead and buried, these posts and interactions are the legacy that will be left behind.

LOTTERY CHAMP

> I won the lottery in 1984 at 18 in NYC, I got 5 of 6 numbers and should have won over $100 thousand.
> The guy in the grocery said it's 5 numbers & the payout is $25 and naive me took it. 😖
> If he didn't cheat me I would have lost my focus to make champion 6 years later.
> God is good 😬
>
> Tweeted by @ChrisEubank

Chris Eubank gained DHOTYA fame in 2018 with an interesting claim that he'd been screwed out of $100,000 of lottery winnings in 1984... in New York. Chris Eubank: not only a former world champion boxer but also a lottery winner in another country. What a man.

The moral of his original tweet was a great one: even with a setback as big as being screwed out of your lottery winnings, you can still achieve great things; and, sometimes, one great thing can distract you from an even greater thing. With that in mind, I decided to post a very tame "didn't happen" claim on DHOTYA, and although Eubank replied with something wacky, he basically reiterated that this story did happen. He'd doubled-down: a DHOTYA fan favourite. Now it didn't matter whether the story was true or not. The nibble was there.

Eubank's last interaction with me was when he publicly challenged me to "combat" and a "dandiness contest". Only Chris Eubank could propose a fight with a Twitter account using the words "challenge you to combat". Now, those of you who know me know that I'm not the most physically gifted, but at the time of the challenge I'd been going to the gym at Warwick Uni for about four months. I googled Eubank's height, age, and weight, and realised I was physically similar to him (except, you know, the world champion bit), and I suspected that I could take a couple of punches before going to hospital.

So, I took the gamble and publicly accepted his request to fight. I even emailed his management to tell them that, despite knowing I'd be dead within 20 seconds, I would fight Eubank in an exhibition boxing match. Of course, I got no reply, and Eubank deleted all of his public interactions with

LOTTERY CHAMP

me. At this point, a "decision-maker" for a well-known British media company reached out to my personal Twitter account to say they'd be interested in sponsoring and broadcasting the fight. Yes, seriously. I'd been offered the equivalent of a decent wedge, and it was all very tempting until I heard these fatal words:

"You and Chris can then both pick a charity to pay your fees to."

LOL, what? You want me, 22-year-old Harry Barnes from Coventry, to skip my 9-5 so I can get smacked up by an ex world champion in front of millions of people (okay, maybe more like 10,000 on a Facebook Live stream), and then you want me to give the money to charity? That money is there to cover three months of unpaid sick leave while I get over my concussion. I've got no idea who people think I am, but having half a million twitter followers does not mean I can throw away 50 grand to a charity. Had they not seen the 2018 housing market? I needed a house deposit!

Needless to say, the fight didn't go ahead. But I never officially turned down the fight, either with Eubank himself or the media company. Let's break this down: Eubank challenged me to a fight, I publicly and privately accepted, and not only did Eubank back out, but he deleted his tweets. Chris Eubank flapped it from me. He was scared. Make no mistake: Chris Eubank backed out of fighting me. If that's not Tinder bio worthy, then nothing is.

As a random side note, I made one of my favourite comments to Eubank during this whole thing. I said: "Calm down Aesop" (in response to Eubank's original tweet being very Aesop fable-ish). I was so proud of remembering who Aesop was from my Year 1 teacher, Mrs. Sibley (RIP), and applying it to real life, but it was barely noticed. I literally sat there waiting for everyone to appreciate it and only about five people did. Thank you to those five people. ♥

SUPERDRY

I was in SuperDry this morning (I got vouchers for Christmas) and I had to travel from Tier 4 where I am now to Tier 2 where there was a SuperDry store open.

So I walk in the shop and a young boy asks me why I'm not wearing a mask. I lean down to him and explain to him that I've worn a mask my entire life, pretending to be comfortable in my own skin. Every time I leave the house, I am nervous about what people will think about my hair, my overweight body, my dry skin, my weird limp, and my arm (one arm is noticeably shorter than the other), and so I told the boy that for the first time in my life, it's everyone else who is wearing the mask and I'm the one not wearing a mask.

He took his mask off, gave me a hug and ran off to his mother and father. I saw them tell him off, and he pointed at me. The family then came out and a blazing row followed. I politely and kindly explained my point, and by the end of it, the entire family took their masks off. We helped each other pick out some items in the store, and I think everyone left that shop a little wiser, and with a sharper look.

What's the point? Talk to people. You might just learn something. 😁

Vauchian/Michael Jamieson via Facebook

Michael Jamieson @MichaelJamieson
Replying to @Vauchian

Ummm, what the hell is this?

Mr Writer @Mr_writer1985
Replying to @Vauchian

I love the fact the first comment is "What the hell is this?"

Chris @chrisross786
Replying to @Vauchian

Someone is going to have to come up with an absolute belter to top this in 2021

Dayo @D1juny
Replying to @Vauchian

The corona virus and other bacterias stood up and clapped while wiping tears off their eyes.

SUPERDRY

It's hard to know where to start with Superdry.

More recent DHOTYA followers will likely remember this one as the runner up in 2021. The post takes so many twists and turns and gets progressively worse as you keep reading. As soon as I read it, I knew it would be a DHOTYA classic, but I didn't anticipate how exactly it was going to play out.

DHOTYA followers are very rarely fans of truly anonymous posts, but this one had been sent to me semi-anonymously, with only "Vauchian", the first name of the original poster on Facebook, being revealed. I knew that the anonymity would wind some followers up, but it was too good not to post, so up it went.

When the awards came around in December 2021, it was one of the bookies' favourites to win the grand prize. In that same year, Twitter had introduced Twitter Spaces, a podcast-style function that allowed a Twitter user to host their own "space", invite guests to speak, and their followers to listen. I thought I'd make the most of this new feature and have a bit of fun during the awards, so I did three nights in a row on Spaces. Ideally, I wanted to reach out to the people who were nominated and get them to talk to us.

On the final night, around the time of the semi-final, "Vauchian" appeared and was desperate to speak. I'd had a couple of DMs tell me they'd done some digging and discovered that Vauchian wasn't real; that it was actually a parody intent on winning DHOTYA. It had made for some great entertainment that night, and eventually we let Vauchian attempt to justify their atrocious lie.

Vauchian talked us through the story, still adamant it was all true, but then the interrogation came. Now, personally, I'm a logical thinker, so I love finding holes in stories, but there just so happened to be an ITV News journalist listening who wanted to contribute too. I honestly can't remember her name (sorry!) but it was first-class entertainment. Then, after a small tip-off from an anonymous user, I found out who Vauchian really was... Michael Jamieson (a random guy, not the Scottish Olympic silver medallist.)

In a YouTube video recorded by Michael/Vauchian, you can pinpoint the exact moment he had to give in and admit who he really was. This was after about one to two hours of trying to convince us of the story's authenticity. Michael admitted he had never heard of DHOTYA and that the post was intended as satire rather than an attempt to be submitted. Once he'd realised he was nominated for the end of year awards, however, he'd started following DHOTYA and even had a £10 bet on himself to win.

Michael uploaded video footage of the debate onto Youtube on New Year's Day 2022, and it really does make for a great watch. This type of content is exactly what DHOTYA is there for- exposing lies on the internet for comedic purposes-and I really do believe we delivered that day on Twitter Spaces.

HELICOPTER - TOM ZANETTI

Met one of the worst examples of a jobsworth arsehole in London today. Long story short i couldn't find my tickets, panicked as train was gonna leave and he didn't let me on it. So within an hour of it leaving the platform I got a helicopter to take me. Fuck you ya lil jellybean

Tom Zanetti via Twitter, @TomZanettiTZ

Tom Zanetti ✔
@TomZanettiTZ

Met one of the worst examples of a jobsworth arsehole in London today. Long story short i couldn't find my tickets, panicked as train was gonna leave and he didn't let me on it. So within an hour of it leaving the platform I got a helicopter to take me. Fuck you ya lil jellybean

Photo:
@TomZanettiTZ

This book is so literally class I had to get a pic with it and get everyone on it. I'm not even a keen reader usually but I swear you won't be able to put this down. It's funny as fuck and if you like snatch / this is England type reads you are going to love it. Nine Foot Tall needs to be a film!!! Search the book now to order it yourself! Put your phone down, read a chapte each night and thank me later!!x

Tom Zanetti via Facebook

Photo:
Tom Zanetti

ROOF - TOM ZANETTI

Just woke up on roof

Tom Zanetti via Snapchat

Just woke up on roof

Photo:
Tom Zanetti

Photo:
@IanRatcliffe21

Ian Ratcliffe @IanRatcliffe21

Afternoon session done! Half time break of the World Darts Championship all-dayer!

@_DHOTYA @TomZanettiTZ

TOM ZANETTI

This was the incident that really made DHOTYA take off... Tom Zanetti.

On 23rd July 2018, only six months after taking over the account, a follower tagged me in a tweet by the singer/DJ Tom Zanetti, who had been flaunting a bit of a "Do you know who I am?" attitude.

In what's possibly the most famous DHOTYA entry of all time, Tom describes a train conductor as "one of the worst examples of a jobsworth arsehole" after he fails to present his ticket to them on a Virgin train from Leeds to London. He then goes on to tell everyone that he had his mate's helicopter on standby anyway.

In his follow-up tweets, Tom even claims that Virgin Trains temporarily banned him from using their services as a result of his outbursts. That "lil jellybean" of a train conductor must have been gutted.

Except... none of this happened. After Tom was exposed on DHOTYA, a follower named Danny tagged Virgin Trains (via their verified Twitter account), and Virgin confirmed: "[We] don't operate from Leeds to London, Danny. We also wouldn't issue 'temporary bans' in this way." And what a shame it'd be if somebody had also found the flight log for the helicopter that Tom claimed to have been on... You've guessed it, somebody did. That helicopter

TOM ZANETTI

did not fly from Leeds to London on that day.

Open and shut case, right? The train he claimed to have been banned from doesn't exist, temporary bans for Virgin Trains don't exist, and the helicopter did exist but didn't make the flight that he claimed it did. Tom should probably just stay quiet, accept that he's been found out, and take the free publicity, right?

Wrong.

23rd July 2018, 16:49 GMT, @TomZanettiTZ pops into the DHOTYA DMs:

"Hahahaha wtf tho bro I'm actually not lying and it did happen HAHAHAHA" 😩😩

Less than two hours later, Tom had sent me two videos of him on a helicopter in an effort to convince me to delete the tweet exposing his original. I responded with a screenshot of the analytics for my original tweet, showing more than 97,000 views, and mockingly encouraged him to embrace the publicity as "not even [his] agent did that" for him.

Lots of DMs (that I'll keep private) went back and forth over several days, including with my personal Twitter, which ultimately resulted in Tom blocking me on not one but two accounts.

Fast-forward to 2019, it's 1am on a Saturday night at Creamfields, and I've found myself alone after

TOM ZANETTI

losing my mates. I end up at a Holy Goof set in one of the tents and bump into some Geordies who take me into their group. I can't remember how, but Tom Zanetti came up in conversation and somebody referenced "that Didn't Happen of the Year account", which I obviously went on to confirm was me. They then go on to tell me about their mate Tommy who's asleep in a tent and who I have to meet. I did, and this led to me meeting a very good friend of mine today: Cerys. I had to get Cerys into this book somehow, so the Tom Zanetti connection is how and where. It's my book and I'll do what I want, okay?

Going into this interaction with Tom, I didn't actually know who he was, although I did recognise his song "You Want Me", which went on to become an ironic pre-drinks song if me and my mates ever wanted a laugh before a night out. Having learned a little bit more about him, I figured that Tom's image was to (seemingly intentionally) show off and be a bit arrogant, and to be fair to him, why not? He's presumably a millionaire and a famous DJ, he's loved by many (especially in his own city of Leeds), and he entertains millions of people. But then again, you could say the same of Jimmy Savile.

GET BREXIT DONE

Let me take you back to early 2019. We're pre-Brexit but post-Brexit referendum, and I'm volunteering as a coach for an U13's football team. The then-Prime Minister, Theresa May, is under a lot of pressure from Brexit voters and MPs to deliver on Brexit, and it's plastered all over the news.

During this, Conservative MP Owen Paterson appears on the news with what feels like a very plausible story: a constituent of his spots him on the London Underground and tells him that he needs to get Brexit done. A Brexit-supporting MP having a Brexit supporter tell him to "get Brexit done" during a very passionate time? Very possible, no doubt.

Then, Labour MP Louise Haigh quotes the video on Twitter and tags DHOTYA, therefore nominating Owen in the process. In reality, I had no intention of actually calling bullshit on Owen's story, as there wasn't really a reason to and, in hindsight, it was quite a poor shout from Louise. Then again, I also didn't care, and having a Labour MP nominate a Conservative MP for DIIOTYA in the middle of very tense political times was great for DHOTYA. It felt like an opportunity I couldn't miss.

In response, I quoted Louise's tweet and jokingly said (but secretly hoped she might actually do it) that I'd donate £50 to charity if she referenced DHOTYA in Parliament during some kind of debate. She (also presumably tongue-in-cheek) replied "Deal".

I thought that was it; a funny bit of interaction. DHOTYA followers loved it, job well done. But I was wrong: 24 hours later I finished work and went to football training, leaving my phone in my jacket on the side of the pitch. One hour later, I checked my phone...

GET BREXIT DONE

1k+ notifications. I'm not sure if anybody can relate to getting 1k+ notifications in an hour, but it's a very scary moment. It's like every bad thing you've ever done in your life flashes before your eyes. It turned out, however, that Owen Paterson had responded in the best way possible.

In an official letter on Houses of Parliament letter-headed paper, Owen demanded that Louise withdraw her nomination for DHOTYA and apologise to him. The letter was posted to Twitter and both Louise and the DHOTYA account were tagged. What makes this more incredible is that this was posted barely an hour before an emergency Brexit press conference, yet all Owen could think about was his DHOTYA nomination.

I'm pretty sure that I'll print that letter out one day and frame it as a fond memory of how far the account has come.

RT HON OWEN PATERSON MP

HOUSE OF COMMONS
LONDON SW1A 0AA

Louise Haigh MP
House of Commons
London
SW1A 0AA

20th March 2019

I note that on Twitter yesterday you nominated my comments about being approached by a member of the public on the London Underground for the "Didn't Happen of the Year" Awards.

On Monday, a man came up to me unprompted and encouraged me to continue my public comments urging the Government to deliver Brexit on time.

I am surprised that you did not discuss the matter with me before publicising your stunt. As I said in the House earlier, the gentleman in question even gave me his card. I will not, of course, publish his name as he gave it to me privately, but you are most welcome to come to my office and see it for yourself. I should, therefore, be grateful if you would withdraw your nomination publicly.

Yours ever,

The Rt Hon Owen Paterson MP

Photo:
Owen Paterson

THE KIDS
ARE ALRIGHT

This is what we live for. You probably have your own assumptions about why we're all here: maybe it's to progress humanity, maybe it's to please a god of some sorts, or maybe us being here is one big accident and there's no meaning to it at all.

But that's where you're wrong... you're alive to witness content like the next few DHOTYA entries, where an 8-year-old's political commentary made their parents weep, and where 60 teenage boys turn out to be the biggest feminist icons you've ever seen.

In what's probably the most famous DHOTYA category, you'll see some posts that will make you question your own children. You'll be sitting on the sofa browsing through this while your 11-year-old is watching KSI videos on YouTube, and you'll never be able to look at them the same again. They'll just never be as good as the children of Twitter who are developing growth mindset apps. Never.

And it's all your fault, you bad parent.

BE A ZELENSKY

Hear hear. As my 6 year old said this morning: "In a world full of Will Smiths, be a Zelensky."

Tweeted by @relaxi777

 Matt Skaife @MartNUFC
Replying to @relaxi777

When I was 4, Bill Clinton was elected 42nd President of the USA. I turned to Father and said. You watch Father, he'll create 22 million jobs but perversion will be his downfall. Father remarked, we shall see.

I napped.

Father kicked my rabbit in the face.

It was a full moon.

May @GruSue
Replying to @relaxi777

I'd like to Will Smith him.

So I asked my husband why people have stopped caring about Brexit. Our son walked in and said: "It's not so much that people have stopped caring about Brexit; I fear that Brexit has stopped caring about the people."
We looked at the floor and wept. He's right you know. He's only 8.

Tweeted by Anon

 Victoria @VickyAllover
Replying to Anon

The clue that this definitely didn't happen, was the utter bullshit that started, made up the main body, then finished the tweet.

B **Bielsa's Cheese Wedge Ultras @Allcheese1**
Replying to Anon

The competition this year is levels above anything we've had previously.

There'll be bloodshed when the voting opens.

DADDY LEFT YOU

My 2 year old woke me with breakfast in bed and said to me "Happy Mother's Day Mommy, just because Daddy left you it doesn't make you less of a woman. You are a everything and more." Agg guys, I am in tears. 😊😂😂😂 🖤🖤🖤

Tweeted by @GakeJole

Nyana Cortez @Nyana_
Replying to @GakeJole

He prepared his famous eggs florentine with hollandaise sauce, turkey bacon, and a side of pumpernickel toast with boysenberry jam.

Georgie @LoneGeorgie
Replying to @GakeJole

Fam, when I was 2 I couldn't even put the square block in the square hole.

SE4coys @SE4coys
Replying to @GakeJole

The only thing missing is all their pets applauding.

George Chilvers @Garswoodlatic
Replying to @GakeJole

I'm calling bulls**t on this. What this story doesn't tell you is that the 2-year-old didn't actually cook the breakfast himself.

He drove to McDonalds and bought a bacon McMuffin and hash brown.

David Henderson @Toonhendy
Replying to @GakeJole

My four year old just cried because I took a balloon off him and he had also shat himself a bit.

What am I doing wrong?

ELON MUSK

Our family was supposed to go on a trip to Disneyland today but when I went to wake our 6 year-old daughter I found this. She refuses to get up. We've been saving for this trip for years. Elon Musk ruined our family vacation and shattered our kids' dreams. #ElonMuskTwitter

Tweeted by @HollyBriden

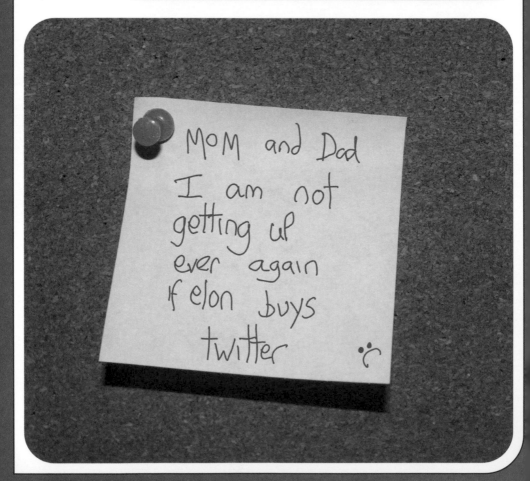

And Brook @mrandrewbrook
Replying to @HollyBriden

It's true, I was the last coat of paint on that door.

StrangeViolet @StrangeViolet
Replying to @HollyBriden

100% didn't happen. A six year old did not write that. A six year old wouldn't understand the concept of owning Twitter. Nor would a six year old understand the concept of Elon Musk.

FEMINISM ... SUFFRAGETTES!

I'm a feminist but… when walking past a boys secondary school today one of the boys called for me to throw their football back over the very high fence.

I responded "there's no way I can get it over that fence"

To which he said "but feminism miss - use your girl power"

60 teenage boys then gathered on the other side of the fence shouting encouragement and chanted "feminism, suffragettes" while I repeatedly attempted the throw and then cheered and applauded when I succeeded.

The kids are alright!

Tweeted by Rose

Todd Bartley @ToddBartley1
Replying to Rose

Didn't happen of the year champions league quality.

Jake Barker @JakeBarker1212
Replying to Rose

Teenage boys who play football are known for their support for feminism to be fair. No surprise to see cheers and applause!

Shoes Buttback @DanMakesNoises
Replying to Rose

If one of the kids had shouted, "You, madam, are the reincarnated embodiment of Emmeline Pankhurst!" then the entire universe would have exploded."

FEMINISM ... SUFFRAGETTES!

If you're reading this, there's a good chance you've already read Rose's tweet on the other page. Please take a moment to go back and properly pay attention. I don't know how deep into the book the editors are going to put this, but there's a chance you're skimming over the entries now. Properly re-read this entry and tell me it's not some of the biggest bullshit you've ever read.

60 teenage boys in an all boys school chanting about feminism and suffragettes. "But feminism Miss" is one of my favourite lines from any DHOTYA entry, and every time I read it I just imagine Oliver Twist begging for more gruel.

Of course there was a round of applause and cheering, too. To be fair, in this context, it's probably the only likely thing to have happened once she'd returned the ball. I really thought that this one could have gone on to win, but the people spoke and it didn't, so hey ho.

Other than declaring this to be one of my top 10 of all time, there's not a huge amount of backstory I can give. I'm conscious this book cost you either £10 pre-Christmas 2022 or £1.00 in the WH Smith clearance basket from January 2023 onwards (or I gave you a copy in a nightclub in 2024 in an attempt to stay relevant), so I feel the need to offer a joke to you; some value for your money.

How do you keep an idiot waiting?

THE TALENT DOCTOR

PROUD DAD MOMENT

So I picked the little dude up yesterday, and as soon as he climbed in the Audi he said & I quote…

Ollie - "Dad, I need to go to your office, I've designed a GROWTH MINDSET APP… I need to plan this and get it wrote down for you…

Me - "Any ideas who your target market is yet son?"

Ollie - "Yep dad, its obvious pioneering kids like me"

I certainly didn't think like that at seven years of age!

#LegendInTheMaking
#ProudDad

TalentDoctorTM Ty Whitehead, via LinkedIn

If you have a child under the age of 13, let alone 7, go and ask them what a Growth Mindset App is, and even better, if they could develop one.

Let's not pretend that this post wasn't posted with the intent to promote "The Audi", as opposed to "The Lambo" or "The Jag" that he probably had to choose between, which I'm sure feature in other LinkedIn posts that definitely aren't all about self-promotion.

BOOKS

Me: How much does it costs to borrow a thousand books from the library?

Small boy: $500?

Smaller girl: $1000!

Me: It's free!

Six hundred kids in the hall gasp, then cheer.

Tweeted by @Jackie_French_

This isn't Matilda; I can 100% promise you that 600 children are not gasping and cheering at the concept that library books are free.

For this to happen, you'd have to assume that most, if not all, of the 600 children did not have any prior knowledge of the concept of a library for this to be such a shocking revelation. Also, any child who did not previously have any knowledge of libraries is not excited upon discovering their existence - those children don't read books.

And are libraries really "free" anyway? There are some really smart children featured in this book who could probably argue the economics of libraries and their sources of funding to find that somebody pays for these things.

DID HAPPEN
OF THE YEAR

I'm well aware there's a chance that one or two of the stories in this book did actually happen, and that they were just so unlikely that I, along with most of the internet, didn't believe they did.

With that in mind, I wanted to give DHOTYA followers an opportunity to share some stories that did happen to them; ones that are so unbelievable that if you'd read them out of context you'd probably have nominated them.

There are some absolutely wild stories here, all posted with consent, but I definitely question the judgement of some of the authors for letting these feature in a book that at least five people will read.

TOY GUN

I have ADHD and I'm quite immature, this happened when I was 15 (now 19, so 4 years ago.) I was out with my girlfriend and her mother when we went to poundland (well known shop for all things £1) and I bought a plastic gun that shot rubber bullets. I was waving it around, again immature, pretending to shoot her and her mum. Got on the bus to go home and her mum shouted up to me that someone has called the police. A few stops later we get to a stop surrounded by police cars and vans, when armed police storm the bus come upstairs pointing guns at me because of a fucking toy. I was then handcuffed, taken off the bus, made to stand against the wall and was searched. The police had a fun laugh out of it when they found the toy, apologised for the inconvenience and let me go

Tweeted by @M1ghtyl10n

PILOT

I flew a charter jet from Abu Dhabi to Grozny with the Chechen prime minister on board with islamic relics which were being loaned for a week to celebrate the opening of a new mosque. I did not have a visa to enter the country but the prime ministers aid told me no problems they would sort on the ground, I was detained and interrogated for 2 days for being a spy, then was supplied copious amounts of alcohol for a further 3 days until we flew out again.

Tweeted by @MillensDartClub

Off to Namibia soon, which reminds me of my last trip there a few years ago. I went via Walvis and was standing in the passport control queue when I started chatting to a British guy behind me. He was quite short and looked to be a backpacker.

It was his first time there and as I was born in the country I was singing its praises and giving him some travel tips. He was a hell of a nice guy and I asked if he needed a lift anywhere as I had someone picking me up. He declined and said he'd make a plan.

Once I got through security an elderly lady approached me for my autograph. I replied in shock saying "I don't even get that in South Africa!"

She looked a bit shocked and said "South Africa!?? Oh I think I've got the wrong person" and walked off…

When I got to the woman who was fetching me, her jaw was practically on the floor staring at my backpacker mate, who minutes earlier I offered a lift to.

There was a lady spritzing his face with water because of the heat.

Turns out it was Tom Hardy, jetting in for Mad Max.

Tweeted by @DerekAlberts1, Derek Alberts

THONG STORY

Mate of mine got arrested in Kavos for streaking down the main strip in a faulty musical parrot thong that would sqwark at random 30 second intervals after it got wet on a previous outing in the sea.

4 lads bombed off down the strip in various comical attire for a laugh and only three came back after they ran past a police cruiser at a petrol station. The other was caught, frisked on the strip wearing only the thong, and taken off to the hills by armed police who intimidated him all the way to the station by sitting on his knee whilst messing with their guns and calling him "bitch".

When he got to the station he had to sit in reception for three hours whilst they checked his passport details, all the while his thong was sqwarking away every time someone in the building strolled past.

We phoned Thomas Cook to find out what we should do and they informed us that he would be let out in the morning after he'd been up before a judge who would prob give him a fine (gave us a laugh imagining him addressing the judge in his feathered thong) and eventually made a judgement call to go out and get wasted on his behalf. We forgot to leave him clothes out assuming he was staying the night so when, after passport checks, the police decided to let him off with a caution, he had to knock on a random neighbours appartment and ask for a t-shirt and shorts.

He found us an hour later outside a kebab shop watching three women in a knife fight with the kebab shop staff, thoroughly pissed off that not only had we gone out on the piss but that we hadn't thought he might get out and need some clothes.

We were more upset he never went into court in that thong.

Tweeted by @DespicableHalzE

SIXTH FORMER AND TEACHER

Sharing a true story for your book.

I went to a Roman Catholic secondary school. At the end of year 7, I went on school residential trip the Netherlands. On the coach I was sat behind a male teacher and female sixth former who seemed very close.

Towards the end of the trip, one morning me and some mates were playing football in the hotel carpark and accidentally hit a parked car. The teacher confiscated the ball and said to come get it at lunchtime. At lunchtime, I was the one picked to go get the ball and without thinking just burst into the teachers room and found him and the sixth former in bed together. Ours eyes locked, I grabbed the ball and legged it. He said never said anything to me but the following term my marks in his class rocketed but wasn't putting in any more effort and began to think he was trying to keep me sweet. I decided to put my theory to the test and regularly handed in utter crap but got top marks. This carried on for 2 years until the guy suddenly disappeared one day. It turned out the affair with the sixth former (who'd since left school) had come to light. It came to light as the teacher was in a relationship with a colleague at the school, who was the sixth formers mother!, the dirty git was seeing both mum and daughter at the same time and she came home early one day and caught them. He never worked in teaching again, married the girl a few years later and last I heard they were still married almost 30 years later

Tweeted by @AlexGunn1981, Alex Gunn

PIGEON LIGHTSABER

I saw a little kid hit a pigeon (hard!) with a toy lightsaber… pigeon was stunned and didn't move, and everyone who witnessed it kinda stopped and stared at the kid. His mum was clearly mortified and had no idea what to do or say, eventually settling on "say sorry to the pigeon!"
It was a weirdly surreal.

Tweeted by Faye Burrows, @FayeAlz

RUN OVER

I got run over by the same car, at the same place, one week later.

Tweeted by @iamjimpage

I was once arrested for setting fire to a police station. I genuinely didn't know it was a police station despite the fact there were police cars outside, I set fire to shedded documents, and in the light of day it was very clearly a police station. In my defence it was cold out.

Further info, me and a mate were staying at another mates house 30 odd miles away (One of Brightons neighbouring towns). We got kicked out of a club in Brighton, too drunk, no trouble! So got a cab back to this mates house, tried to break in but it wasn't happening. Think it was February, so on the coast it was freezing. Saw an open garage so used it for shelter. Still cold. Police car outside, some reason it didn't click, maybe we thought it was a garage, no idea. Wheelie bin full of shredded paper looked warm, set it on fire. Within 2 mins police came so we split and ran. I ran the wrong way, into the stations walled car park, my mate ran the other way and hid under a car for 30 mins or so before a sniffer dog found him.

Obviously our stories tallied up and we got away with it, we were told we'd have to pay for damages but the bill never came, we did have to go to Lewes fire station to do fire awareness courses, 2 or 3 hour sessions. This might sound ok, but we were 25 at the time and every other kid, yes kid, was about 16. I thought I'd kept this secret from my family until it took centre stage on my best man's speech.

Tweeted by @Juppopovic, Dar

DI MATTEO

I once played five-a-side with Roberto De Matteo. He set me up for a tap-in and high-fives me after I scored. Someone on the opposing team tried to nutmeg him. Next chance he got, De Matteo two-footed him into the wall. Two weeks later, he scored after 40 secs in the FA Cup Final.

Tweeted by @MrPerson77, Matt

BUS EGG

When I was a kid I threw an egg at a passing bus from about 30 yards. The pane of glass it hit was the seat where my Mum was sat at. If the glass wasn't there, the egg would of smashed right in her face. The only time in years she rode on the bus as well.

Tweeted by @TommyTash1

Me and a friend broke into a Royal Mail van when drunk after clubbing. It was early hours of the morning and we passed the depot on the way to his house after getting off the night bus. We went into the open car park where all the vans were lined up and quickly noticed they all had the keys in it them. I started driving it round the depot car park trying to do skids and handbrake turns while my friend was in the back opening post from the sacks looking for birthday money/gyros. I crashed the van into a wall, threw up and ran away to his house. Next day we got nicked and was facing charges. Both of us stubbornly denied it and because the council cctv wasn't clear enough to positively identify us (2001) we both received a generic formal caution but no further action on the more serious things. 1000% true but sounds as if it isn't.

Tweeted by Billy

 Didn't Happen of the Year Awards @_DHOTYA
Replying to Billy

Mate thats amazing, did they not test your vomit for DNA or was that a bit too long ago for them to really do that?

 Billy
Replying to @_DHOTYA

No DNA testing. It wasn't even brought up. I was surprised too because I threw up where I wasn't wearing a belt so when I hit the wall the wheel hit me in the stomach causing me to puke. Just wasn't mentioned.

PIGEON ATTACK

I once had a pigeon nesting issue on my balcony and one night after shooing one away I had reached my limit and stormed to B&Q to buy some netting. As I walked through the aisles looking for what I needed a pigeon flew out of one of the shelves and knocked me to the floor.

Tweeted by @EraserOfficial, "Alex"

Didn't Happen of the Year Awards @_DHOTYA
Replying to @EraserOfficial, "Alex"

Seriously? Was the pigeon really that strong yeah?

@EraserOfficial, "Alex"
Replying to @_DHOTYA

Yeah no joke - it was probably more of a case of it flying into my face and me falling backwards from the shock but yeah… bad times.

AND THE
WINNER IS...

This really should be the best chapter of them all, as you're about to see the winners of DHOTYA from 2016-2021, as voted for by the DHOTYA followers themselves.

Some absolute classics to read here, all the way from Keith's Brexit-voting mum to an English-speaking person using the word "supermarche" like they've just got off the ferry in Calais.

In advance, I really am sorry that you had to read Supermarche. It's one of the best and worst things you've ever read at the same time. Some people did win money on it that year though, and the bookies lost big time having priced it around 8/1 to win.

KEITH'S MUM (2016)

> Just took 93yr Mum to vote, she's registered blind. In a very loud voice she said, "Which box for out?" A cheer went up from the waiting voters.
>
> Keith Adams, @keitheadams

The original DHOTYA, the 2016 winner... Keith's Mum. This is the Ground Zero for DHOTYA.

On reflection, this might not even get to the final of a modern day DHOTYA. When this won in 2016, DHOTYA wasn't in its current format: it was being run from the founder's Twitter account, @weahscousin, and the post had been selected as part of some fun tournament. With over 400,000 followers, and many more aware of DHOTYA without following it, only the best of the best get submitted nowadays.

However, without Keith's Mum, I don't think DHOTYA would even exist. Or, at least, it wouldn't be as popular as it is today. It's gone on to become a 'copypasta' (a template for other people to create spoofs) and it often comes up during UK elections, including the last two general elections.

Keith went on to delete his Twitter account a year or so after posting this, but his mum would be 99 now, so let's hope that she's about to get a letter from the King.

#PROUDAUNTIEMOMENT (2017)

My 11 year old nephew just said that he doesn't like James Bond because he saw a cover of a James Bond book with a naked woman on and he didn't think that women's bodies should be used to sell things #proudauntiemoment

Amelia Womack @Amelia_Womack via Twitter

Proud Auntie Moment was the entry that started the more controversial era of DHOTYA, as it was the first time someone expressed a concern about their post being called out.

To set the scene, this winner came at a time when DHOTYA had around 20k followers and was starting to receive a bit of attention, with the 2017 awards being a huge success with the early followers.

But there's a moment in everyone's life when they realise how journalism actually works, and this was that moment for me. You eventually figure out that the majority of journalists have zero integrity and are just desperate to get themselves published, and this post made me realise that I should never, ever trust them. You hear a lot of celebrities, politicians and sports stars say similar things, but I think you never truly believe it until you've experienced a small piece of it.

There are two Amelias in this story: Amelia Womack, the author of this post, and Amelia Tait, a journalist who, back then, was writing for the New Statesman. If I remember correctly, I wasn't aware at the time that Amelia Womack was doubling down on the post; I didn't know that she was adamant that her 11-year-old nephew really was on a James Bond ban because of an attractive woman on one of the book's covers. If I'd known this, I'm sure I would have tried to interact with her on the account.

So, Amelia Tait, whom I'd never heard of, reached out to me about the outcome of DHOTYA 2017. She seemed very positive and upbeat about it, and asked if I had time to speak with her for a New Statesman's article. I'd never done an interview with any kind of media before, and I was actually quite excited, both on a personal level and for the potential exposure for DHOTYA.

#PROUDAUNTIEMOMENT (2017)

Fast forward to my interview, and Amelia Tait is laughing and joking with me, telling me her favourite entry of the year and about how she liked the account and awards. We started to discuss Proud Auntie Moment, and we both agreed that, although we appreciated the humour in it, it wasn't our personal favourite that year. Based on the conversation we'd had, I was expecting a positive review of the account and awards; instead, I was screwed over by an article (in which she'd also spoken to Amelia Womack) which heavily implied a sexist bias behind both the account and the followers' decision to make Proud Auntie Moment the winner.

Lacking the confidence to call her out at the time, I didn't particularly criticise the article when I was asked how I found it. That was, however, until the following year, when I saw a second heavily misleading article from Amelia Tait. This time, she'd brought in an expert to analyse whether the account actually was sexist and whether it had a preference to "target" women.

#PROUDAUNTIEMOMENT (2017)

Amazingly, and without any sense of irony, this article included a look at the past year or so of DHOTYA entries, which Amelia had categorised into male and female before sub-categorising them into "normal people", "celebrities", and so on. After writing an entire article claiming that the account targets women, she'd managed to prove that, in the majority of categories, men were disproportionately posted on DHOTYA by up to 3.5x, and that women were posted more than men in just two categories. Even in those two categories, women had only been posted around 1.6x as much as men.

Despite the article being published without my knowledge or opportunity to comment, I decided to challenge Amelia's standards of journalism. I later received a couple of apologies via DM for how everything was handled, but the article is still live and unamended.

In short, Proud Auntie Moment triggered a journalistic attack on the underlying intent of DHOTYA, only to prove that men actually have a harder time on the account. Basically, don't trust the media.

SUPERMARCHE (2018)

Went into my local supermarche and the asshole at the door says "Good Morning Ma'am". I turn and look at him. "Excuse me?" I said. And he repeated himself. "Who the fuck do you think you are to call me Ma'am, I'll have you know you are pushing gender stereotypes and one of my best friends is struggling with their gender identity at the moment and people like you are the reason they always feel so persecuted. He starts to say he didn't mean anything by it, WRONG ANSWER BUDDY. 20 minutes later and security end up getting called. As they're about to kick me out, another shopper stops them and explains how I'm in the right and a hero for standing up for people. The manager comes out mid-way through this and fires the employee on the spot. Turns out their child is also struggling with gender identity. The manager thanked me and said my next shopping trip there is free. Always stand up for what you think is right and karma will reward you!

Anonymous post from Facebook

Jonny Wilson @jonnypwilson

Replying to anonymous

"I turn and look at HIM." ... lol

Benny @BenzlWashington

Replying to anonymous

Real or not ... Saying Supermarche is next level pretentiousness.

Conrad @conradk71

Replying to anonymous

My 93 year old mother was there and gave out a loud cheer.

Clare de Lune @isacatabeast

Replying to anonymous

And then the employee sued for wrongful dismissal, won a large payout, and this is why Tescos can't afford to stock aubergines any more.

SUPERMARCHE (2018)

How fucking mental is what you've just read? It gets worse every single time you read it.

It reminds me of all those Hollywood actors singing John Lennon's "Imagine" during the first COVID lockdown: you get angrier every time you watch it until you just have to laugh at how bonkers it is.

Intending to submit it anonymously, Supermarche was sent to me with the name blurred out.

It went on to comfortably win DHOTYA 2018, and is many people's absolute favourite entry.

This post was also the start of the public hatred for anonymous entries, as people in 2018 loved to reply directly.

HE'S ONLY ONE (2019)

Y'all my son woke me up out my sleep crying and said. "Mommy I know you're tired of working, trying to make it better for me and my sister. I'll go to work for you today."
This made me cry 🫠
He's only 1.

Jai Janayia via Facebook

Photo: Jai Janayia

AND THE WINNER IS…

HE'S ONLY ONE (2019)

The DHOTYA 2019 winner, He's Only 1. Iconic.

At the time of writing this, I know Meze Publishing are discussing whether the photo of the child in this could/should be published. I guess we're about to find out whether the lawyers here are cool.

The reason I mention that is because the picture is what makes this post a success. I do get it if it can't be published though, so I'd encourage you to use Twitter to search for "He's Only 1". The photo is basically a one-year-old in his mum's work uniform, name tag and all, sobbing, who's blatantly been made to dress this way by his mum for a social media post.

Let's change the tone of this a bit to acknowledge how mental that actually is and how often parents exploit their children on social media for clout. Sometimes they're just referencing them in their tweets (maybe nameless, photoless, etc.), but too often they're named and photographed. Poor kid.

Those who follow the awards on Twitter will know that, each year, I get my friend Jack Brownridge to make a photo for the winner, usually with my creative direction. I had a few friends working at B&Q at the time, so I put a kid in a B&Q uniform in the bathroom department. Three years later, that image still makes me laugh every time I see it.

I've never heard from the author here, though there is a conspiracy theory among some followers that it was a piss-take. There could be some truth behind that, but I don't know if we'll ever know. All we know is that it didn't actually happen, which is literally the point of the account, so I can live with that.

THE VOICELESS (2020)

Need to share, me and my 6yr old Charlie were just shopping at Asda and people werent keeping there distance and staff werent doing nothing so Charlie got out the line and shouted "everyone needs to keep 2 meteres apart at all times". then to make me even more proud he took all the olderly people out the line and took them all to the front, a woman in the que shouted "we were waiting first". without thinking Charlie said "with respect mam, this disease is taking away our mothers, fathers, grandmothers, grandfathers. we need to do all we can to protect them as they are the most vulnerable and this disease is spreading fast. i am sure your there lives are more important than your shopping so think with your head and not your heart and be the change you want to see in the world" suddenly you hear people in the que gasp as they can not believe that somsone of Charlie's age could have so much inteligence and personality, a man in the que turns around and said to me "your son is going to be the future leader of this country". Charlie overheard and came over and said "excuse me sir with respect I do not want fame or money. My happiness does not come from a job or money it comes from being the voice of the voiceless".

I can not be more proud of my son. I needed to share, not to brag for awareness.

Anonymously posted to the Eastbourne Echo on Facebook

I really don't think there's anything I can say about The Voiceless to make this even better. Just read it, and read it again, and try not to cry.

If you're a parent, just know that you'll never be even half the parent that this original poster on Facebook is. Look how great her children are. Yours? Doesn't even know how to spell "Voiceless".

ALMONDS (2021)

Today, I was eating almonds on a bench in the park, and a lady walked by and started yelling at me.

"You should NOT be eating almonds. I have a severe allergy and so does my son."

Without saying anything, I calmly reached into my yellow purse and took out my new essential oil blend. Then I stood up, still without saying anything, and injected her and her son with the blend with the needle that I keep in my purse for situations like this (it happens more often than you'd think 😄) then I gave her an almond and told her to eat it. After she finished she told me she had several doctors prescribe her medication for her allergy and none of them actually worked, but mine did! 😄 she actually asked me if I was literally a doctor, and when I told her I wasn't her jaw dropped

"You aren't???"

"Nnnnnope!" I said smugly

So today, not only did I get a new customer for my blend, but I also got £100 as an apology for her bothering me! She also asked for the rest of the bag of almonds 😄

Anonymous via Facebook

Convincing John @JohnQJesus

Replying to anonymous

£100 quid? Is that all?

When I injected my special blend into a woman and her kid that time, I got six years and a lifetime ban from Alton Towers.

Andrew wilson @Andrewwilson87

Replying to anonymous

To be fair, a women that protective of her son is almost certainly not going to have an issue with a stranger just injecting them with an unknown substance from a potential used needle. Entirely plausible.

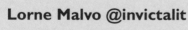

Lorne Malvo @invictalit

Replying to anonymous

And I am now on remand having been arrested for injecting two total strangers with what is actually drain cleaner.

ALMONDS (2021)

Almonds has gone on to become one of the best DHOTYA entries of all time. Even as I type this, I've literally just posted the announcement for The DHOTYA Shield 2022, a vote which determines the fans' favourite ever entry.

It'll be coming up against The Voiceless, which is the current Greatest Of All Time (GOAT) and reigning DHOTYA Shield holder, but as the winner of DHOTYA 2021, Almonds has a shot at being the new GOAT.

So what about Almonds makes it so good?

The absolute audacity of Almonds is what makes it so good. It's so good that it makes you question one, or all, of these things:

Is it satire and the author is just having a laugh?

Is the author okay? Do they need some help in any way?

Is the child okay if this, in some crazy parallel universe, actually happened?

It's a proper story, with elements of Supermarche and The Voiceless, and it just gets better and better as it goes on. It's so unrealistic that it goes past the assumption that the author is just taking the piss, and instead brings you back to asking if the author is genuinely trying to convince people that this actually happened.

One of the craziest things you'll read on the internet, or in a book, ever. Period.

NOPE

DIDN'T HAPPEN
of the **YEAR AWARDS**
#DHOTYA